For Lyrical Lucille

LADYBIRD BOOKS, INC.
Auburn, Maine 04210 U.S.A.
LADYBIRD BOOKS LTD
Loughborough, Leicestershire, England
© EUGENIE FERNANDES 1990

Printed in England

ABC AND YOU

an alphabet book

By Eugenie Fernandes

Ladybird Books

Amazing Amanda

B Brave Ben

 Curious Caroline

D Daring Dan

E

Energetic Emily

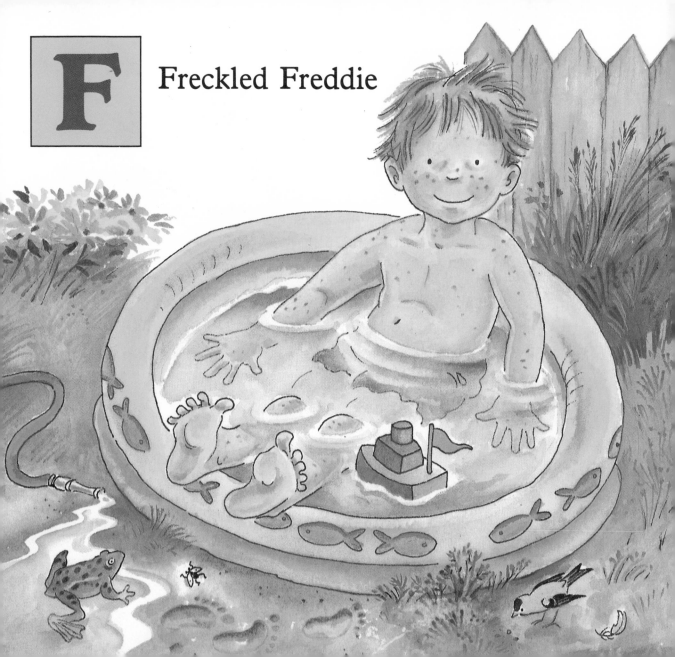

F Freckled Freddie

Graceful Gloria

H Happy Henry

Ill Ida

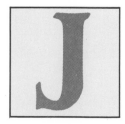

J

Jumping Jennifer

K Kind Kim

L

Little Lucy

M Marvelous Matthew

 Napping Noah

O

Organized Olivia

P

Proud Peter

Q

Quiet Quincy

R

Royal Rosie

Soapy Sylvie

T

Tumbling Toby

U

Unhappy Ursula

V Victorious Vickie

W Wet Walter

Excited Xavier

Y Yawning Yolanda

Z Zippity Zack

... and You!

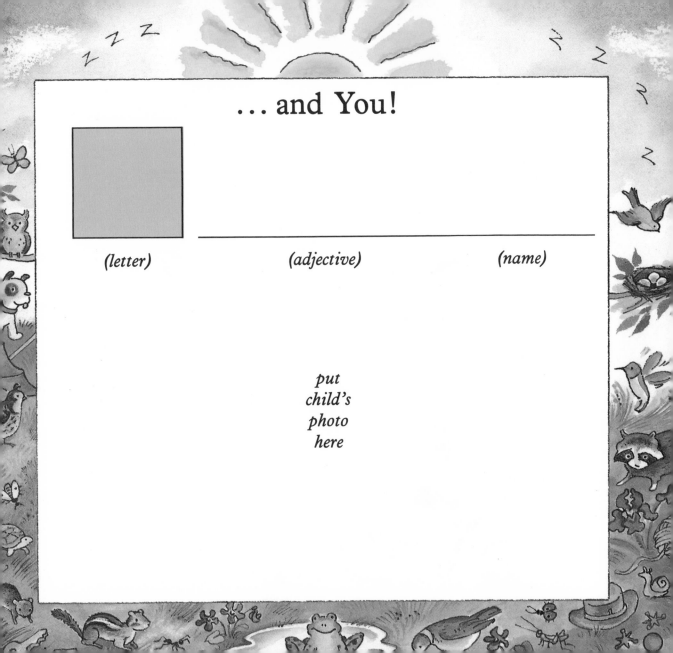

(letter)   (adjective)   (name)

*put
child's
photo
here*